DATE	DESCRIPTION	AMOUNT

DATE	DESCRIPTION	AMOUNT

DATE	DESCRIPTION	AMOUNT

DATE	DESCRIPTION	AMOUNT

DATE	DESCRIPTION	AMOUNT

DATE	DESCRIPTION	AMOUNT

DATE	DESCRIPTION	AMOUNT

DATE	DESCRIPTION	AMOUNT

DATE	DESCRIPTION	AMOUNT

DATE	DESCRIPTION	AMOUNT

DATE	DESCRIPTION	AMOUNT

DATE	DESCRIPTION	AMOUNT

DATE	DESCRIPTION	AMOUNT

DATE	DESCRIPTION	AMOUNT

DATE	DESCRIPTION	AMOUNT

DATE	DESCRIPTION	AMOUNT

DATE	DESCRIPTION	AMOUNT

DATE	DESCRIPTION	AMOUNT

DATE	DESCRIPTION	AMOUNT

DATE	DESCRIPTION	AMOUNT

DATE	DESCRIPTION	AMOUNT

DATE	DESCRIPTION	AMOUNT

DATE	DESCRIPTION	AMOUNT

DATE	DESCRIPTION	AMOUNT

DATE	DESCRIPTION	AMOUNT

DATE	DESCRIPTION	AMOUNT

DATE	DESCRIPTION	AMOUNT

DATE	DESCRIPTION	AMOUNT

DATE	DESCRIPTION	AMOUNT

DATE	DESCRIPTION	AMOUNT

DATE	DESCRIPTION	AMOUNT

DATE	DESCRIPTION	AMOUNT

DATE	DESCRIPTION	AMOUNT

DATE	DESCRIPTION	AMOUNT

DATE	DESCRIPTION	AMOUNT

DATE	DESCRIPTION	AMOUNT

DATE	DESCRIPTION	AMOUNT

DATE	DESCRIPTION	AMOUNT

DATE	DESCRIPTION	AMOUNT

DATE	DESCRIPTION	AMOUNT

DATE	DESCRIPTION	AMOUNT

DATE	DESCRIPTION	AMOUNT

DATE	DESCRIPTION	AMOUNT

DATE	DESCRIPTION	AMOUNT

DATE	DESCRIPTION	AMOUNT

DATE	DESCRIPTION	AMOUNT

DATE	DESCRIPTION	AMOUNT

DATE	DESCRIPTION	AMOUNT

DATE	DESCRIPTION	AMOUNT

DATE	DESCRIPTION	AMOUNT

DATE	DESCRIPTION	AMOUNT

DATE	DESCRIPTION	AMOUNT

DATE	DESCRIPTION	AMOUNT

DATE	DESCRIPTION	AMOUNT

DATE	DESCRIPTION	AMOUNT

DATE	DESCRIPTION	AMOUNT

DATE	DESCRIPTION	AMOUNT

DATE	DESCRIPTION	AMOUNT

DATE	DESCRIPTION	AMOUNT

DATE	DESCRIPTION	AMOUNT

DATE	DESCRIPTION	AMOUNT

DATE	DESCRIPTION	AMOUNT

DATE	DESCRIPTION	AMOUNT

DATE	DESCRIPTION	AMOUNT

DATE	DESCRIPTION	AMOUNT

DATE	DESCRIPTION	AMOUNT

DATE	DESCRIPTION	AMOUNT

DATE	DESCRIPTION	AMOUNT

DATE	DESCRIPTION	AMOUNT

DATE	DESCRIPTION	AMOUNT

DATE	DESCRIPTION	AMOUNT

DATE	DESCRIPTION	AMOUNT

DATE	DESCRIPTION	AMOUNT

DATE	DESCRIPTION	AMOUNT

DATE	DESCRIPTION	AMOUNT

DATE	DESCRIPTION	AMOUNT

DATE	DESCRIPTION	AMOUNT

DATE	DESCRIPTION	AMOUNT

DATE	DESCRIPTION	AMOUNT

DATE	DESCRIPTION	AMOUNT

DATE	DESCRIPTION	AMOUNT

DATE	DESCRIPTION	AMOUNT

DATE	DESCRIPTION	AMOUNT

DATE	DESCRIPTION	AMOUNT

DATE	DESCRIPTION	AMOUNT

DATE	DESCRIPTION	AMOUNT

DATE	DESCRIPTION	AMOUNT

DATE	DESCRIPTION	AMOUNT

DATE	DESCRIPTION	AMOUNT

DATE	DESCRIPTION	AMOUNT

DATE	DESCRIPTION	AMOUNT

DATE	DESCRIPTION	AMOUNT

DATE	DESCRIPTION	AMOUNT

DATE	DESCRIPTION	AMOUNT

DATE	DESCRIPTION	AMOUNT

DATE	DESCRIPTION	AMOUNT

DATE	DESCRIPTION	AMOUNT

DATE	DESCRIPTION	AMOUNT

DATE	DESCRIPTION	AMOUNT

DATE	DESCRIPTION	AMOUNT

www.ingramcontent.com/pod-product-compliance
Lightning Source LLC
Chambersburg PA
CBHW021849170526
45157CB00007B/3003